With Love and Fondest Memories of:

HONORING

Ms. Bee

May there be comfort in knowing someone so special will never be forgotten.

~ Julie Hebert

If I'm having a tough day, my support system includes the following:

30 Things I Can Do To Feel Better

Use this space to create a list of up to 30 activities you can engage in to feel better.

1. ______________________
2. ______________________
3. ______________________
4. ______________________
5. ______________________
6. ______________________
7. ______________________
8. ______________________
9. ______________________
10. ______________________
11. ______________________
12. ______________________
13. ______________________
14. ______________________
15. ______________________
16. ______________________
17. ______________________
18. ______________________
19. ______________________
20. ______________________
21. ______________________
22. ______________________
23. ______________________
24. ______________________
25. ______________________
26. ______________________
27. ______________________
28. ______________________
29. ______________________
30. ______________________

I remember...

____

____

____

____

____

____

____

____

____

____

____

____

____

____

____

____

____

"Although it's difficult today to see beyond the sorrow, May looking back in memory help comfort you tomorrow." ~ Unknown

I remember...

I remember...

If you were here, I'd tell you...

If you were here, I'd tell you...

If you were here, I'd tell you...

If you were here, I'd tell you...

If you were here, I'd tell you...

Date: /   /

If I need support today, I will call:

____

My plans for today are: _________________________

____

____

I'm really missing this about you... ______________

I smiled when I remembered this about you... ____

____

I find it helpful when: _________________________

____

____

I am comforted by: ____________________________

____

____

I feel your presence most when... ____

____

____

Whenever I start to feel overwhelmed by pain, regret or despair, I will... ______________

____

____

I will commit to this activity to help me feel better: ______________________________

____

Use this space to jot down your memory of visitations or dreams about your loved one:

____

____

____

Date: / /

If I need support today, I will call:

____

My plans for today are: _______________________

____

____

I'm really missing this about you... _______________

____

Today I:
- ☐ Feel supported
- ☐ Feel angry
- ☐ Feel like crying
- ☐ Feel lonely
- ☐ Feel tired
- ☐ Feel sad
- ☐ Feel neutral
- ☐ Am taking it minute by minute

I smiled when I remembered this about you... _______________________________________

____

I find it helpful when: _______________________________________

____

____

I am comforted by: _______________________________________

____

____

I feel your presence most when... _______________________________________

____

____

Whenever I start to feel overwhelmed by pain, regret or despair, I will... _______________

____

____

I will commit to this activity to help me feel better: _______________________________

____

Use this space to jot down your memory of visitations or dreams about your loved one:

____

____

____

Date: /   /

If I need support today, I will call:

____

My plans for today are: ________________________

____

____

I'm really missing this about you... ______________

____

I smiled when I remembered this about you... ______________________________________

____

I find it helpful when: ____

____

____

I am comforted by: ____

____

____

I feel your presence most when... ____

____

____

Whenever I start to feel overwhelmed by pain, regret or despair, I will... ____________

____

____

I will commit to this activity to help me feel better: ______________________________

____

Use this space to jot down your memory of visitations or dreams about your loved one:

____

____

____

Date: /   /

If I need support today, I will call:

____

My plans for today are: _______________________

____

____

I'm really missing this about you... _____________

____

I smiled when I remembered this about you... ____________________________________

____

I find it helpful when: ____

____

____

I am comforted by: ____

____

____

I feel your presence most when... ____

____

____

Whenever I start to feel overwhelmed by pain, regret or despair, I will... ______________

____

____

I will commit to this activity to help me feel better: _______________________________

____

Use this space to jot down your memory of visitations or dreams about your loved one:

____

____

____

Date: ___ / ___ / ___

If I need support today, I will call:

____

My plans for today are: ___________________________

____

____

I'm really missing this about you... ___________________

I smiled when I remembered this about you... ____

____

I find it helpful when: ____

____

____

I am comforted by: ____

____

____

I feel your presence most when... ____

____

____

Whenever I start to feel overwhelmed by pain, regret or despair, I will... ___________

____

____

I will commit to this activity to help me feel better: _________________________

____

Use this space to jot down your memory of visitations or dreams about your loved one:

____

____

____

Date: _____ / _____ / _____

If I need support today, I will call:

____

My plans for today are: _______________________

____

____

I'm really missing this about you... _____________

____

I smiled when I remembered this about you... ________________________________

____

I find it helpful when: _________________________

____

____

I am comforted by: ____________________________

____

____

I feel your presence most when... ______________

____

____

Whenever I start to feel overwhelmed by pain, regret or despair, I will... ___________

____

____

I will commit to this activity to help me feel better: ________________________

____

Use this space to jot down your memory of visitations or dreams about your loved one:

____

____

____

Date: / /

If I need support today, I will call:

____

My plans for today are: _______________________

____

____

I'm really missing this about you... _______________

____

I smiled when I remembered this about you... _______________________________________

____

I find it helpful when: _________________________

____

____

I am comforted by: ____________________________

____

____

I feel your presence most when... ________________

____

____

Whenever I start to feel overwhelmed by pain, regret or despair, I will... _______________

____

____

I will commit to this activity to help me feel better: _______________

____

Use this space to jot down your memory of visitations or dreams about your loved one:

____

____

____

Date: /   /

If I need support today, I will call:

____

My plans for today are: _______________________

____

____

I'm really missing this about you... _____________

____

I smiled when I remembered this about you... _______________________________________

____

I find it helpful when: ____

____

____

I am comforted by: ____

____

____

I feel your presence most when... ____

____

____

Whenever I start to feel overwhelmed by pain, regret or despair, I will... _____________

____

____

I will commit to this activity to help me feel better: _______________________________

____

Use this space to jot down your memory of visitations or dreams about your loved one:

____

____

____

Date: / /

If I need support today, I will call:

____

My plans for today are: _______________________

____

____

I'm really missing this about you... _____________

____

I smiled when I remembered this about you... ___________________________________

____

I find it helpful when: ____

____

____

I am comforted by: ____

____

____

I feel your presence most when... ____

____

____

Whenever I start to feel overwhelmed by pain, regret or despair, I will... ___________

____

____

I will commit to this activity to help me feel better: _____________________________

____

Use this space to jot down your memory of visitations or dreams about your loved one:

____

____

____

Date: /   /

If I need support today, I will call:

____

My plans for today are: _________________________

____

____

I'm really missing this about you... ______________

I smiled when I remembered this about you... ____

____

I find it helpful when: ____

____

____

I am comforted by: ____

____

____

I feel your presence most when... ____

____

____

Whenever I start to feel overwhelmed by pain, regret or despair, I will... _______________

____

____

I will commit to this activity to help me feel better: _________________________________

____

Use this space to jot down your memory of visitations or dreams about your loved one:

____

____

____

Date: /   /

If I need support today, I will call:

____

My plans for today are: _______________________

____

____

I'm really missing this about you... ______________

____

I smiled when I remembered this about you... ____

____

I find it helpful when: ____

____

____

I am comforted by: ____

____

____

I feel your presence most when... ____

____

____

Whenever I start to feel overwhelmed by pain, regret or despair, I will... _______________

____

____

I will commit to this activity to help me feel better: _______________________________

____

Use this space to jot down your memory of visitations or dreams about your loved one:

____

____

____

Date: /   /

If I need support today, I will call:

____

My plans for today are: _______________________

____

____

I'm really missing this about you... _______________

____

I smiled when I remembered this about you... _______________________________________

____

I find it helpful when: ____

____

____

I am comforted by: ____

____

____

I feel your presence most when... ____

____

____

Whenever I start to feel overwhelmed by pain, regret or despair, I will... _____________

____

____

I will commit to this activity to help me feel better: _______________________________

____

Use this space to jot down your memory of visitations or dreams about your loved one:

____

____

____

Date: /   /

If I need support today, I will call:

____

My plans for today are: _______________________

____

____

I'm really missing this about you... _______________

____

Today I:

☐ Feel supported
☐ Feel angry
☐ Feel like crying
☐ Feel lonely
☐ Feel tired
☐ Feel sad
☐ Feel neutral
☐ Am taking it minute by minute

I smiled when I remembered this about you... _______________________________

____

I find it helpful when: _______________________________

____

____

I am comforted by: _______________________________

____

____

I feel your presence most when... _______________________________

____

____

Whenever I start to feel overwhelmed by pain, regret or despair, I will... _______________

____

____

I will commit to this activity to help me feel better: _______________________

____

Use this space to jot down your memory of visitations or dreams about your loved one:

____

____

____

Date: / /

If I need support today, I will call:

____

My plans for today are: _______________________

____

____

I'm really missing this about you... _______________

____

<table>
<tr><td>Today I:</td></tr>
<tr><td>☐ Feel supported</td></tr>
<tr><td>☐ Feel angry</td></tr>
<tr><td>☐ Feel like crying</td></tr>
<tr><td>☐ Feel lonely</td></tr>
<tr><td>☐ Feel tired</td></tr>
<tr><td>☐ Feel sad</td></tr>
<tr><td>☐ Feel neutral</td></tr>
<tr><td>☐ Am taking it minute by minute</td></tr>
</table>

I smiled when I remembered this about you... _______________________________

____

I find it helpful when: _______________________________

____

____

I am comforted by: _______________________________

____

____

I feel your presence most when... _______________________________

____

____

Whenever I start to feel overwhelmed by pain, regret or despair, I will... _____________

____

____

I will commit to this activity to help me feel better: _______________________

____

Use this space to jot down your memory of visitations or dreams about your loved one:

____

____

____

Date: / /

If I need support today, I will call:

____

My plans for today are: _______________________________

____

____

I'm really missing this about you... _______________________

I smiled when I remembered this about you... _______________________________________

____

I find it helpful when: _______________________________________

____

____

I am comforted by: _______________________________________

____

____

I feel your presence most when... _______________________________________

____

____

Whenever I start to feel overwhelmed by pain, regret or despair, I will... _______________

____

____

I will commit to this activity to help me feel better: _______________________________

____

Use this space to jot down your memory of visitations or dreams about your loved one:

____

____

____

Date: /   /

If I need support today, I will call:

____

My plans for today are: _______________________

____

____

I'm really missing this about you... _______________

I smiled when I remembered this about you... _______________________________________

____

I find it helpful when: ____

____

____

I am comforted by: ____

____

____

I feel your presence most when... ____

____

____

Whenever I start to feel overwhelmed by pain, regret or despair, I will... _______________

____

____

I will commit to this activity to help me feel better: _______________________________

____

Use this space to jot down your memory of visitations or dreams about your loved one:

____

____

____

Date: / /

If I need support today, I will call:

____

My plans for today are: _________________________

____

____

I'm really missing this about you... _______________

I smiled when I remembered this about you... _______________________________________

____

I find it helpful when: _______________________________________

____

____

I am comforted by: _______________________________________

____

____

I feel your presence most when... _______________________________________

____

____

Whenever I start to feel overwhelmed by pain, regret or despair, I will... _______________

____

____

I will commit to this activity to help me feel better: _______________________________

____

Use this space to jot down your memory of visitations or dreams about your loved one:

____

____

____

Date: /   /

If I need support today, I will call:

____

My plans for today are: _______________________________

____

____

I'm really missing this about you... _______________________

____

I smiled when I remembered this about you... _______________________________

____

I find it helpful when: _________________________________

____

____

I am comforted by: ___________________________________

____

____

I feel your presence most when... _______________________________

____

____

Whenever I start to feel overwhelmed by pain, regret or despair, I will... ____________

____

____

I will commit to this activity to help me feel better: _______________________

____

Use this space to jot down your memory of visitations or dreams about your loved one:

____

____

____

Date: /   /

If I need support today, I will call:

____

My plans for today are: ___________________________

____

____

I'm really missing this about you... ________________

____

I smiled when I remembered this about you... ____

____

I find it helpful when: ____

____

____

I am comforted by: ____

____

____

I feel your presence most when... ____

____

____

Whenever I start to feel overwhelmed by pain, regret or despair, I will... ________________

____

____

I will commit to this activity to help me feel better: ____________________________________

____

Use this space to jot down your memory of visitations or dreams about your loved one:

____

____

____

Today I:

☐ Feel supported
☐ Feel angry
☐ Feel like crying
☐ Feel lonely
☐ Feel tired
☐ Feel sad
☐ Feel neutral
☐ Am taking it minute by minute

Date: /   /

If I need support today, I will call:

____

My plans for today are: _______________________

____

____

I'm really missing this about you... _______________

____

I smiled when I remembered this about you... ________________________________

____

I find it helpful when: ____

____

____

I am comforted by: ____

____

____

I feel your presence most when... ____

____

____

Whenever I start to feel overwhelmed by pain, regret or despair, I will... ___________

____

____

I will commit to this activity to help me feel better: ______________________________

____

Use this space to jot down your memory of visitations or dreams about your loved one:

____

____

____

Date: /   /

If I need support today, I will call:

____

My plans for today are: _________________

____

____

I'm really missing this about you... _________

____

<table>
<tr><td>Today I:</td></tr>
<tr><td>☐ Feel supported</td></tr>
<tr><td>☐ Feel angry</td></tr>
<tr><td>☐ Feel like crying</td></tr>
<tr><td>☐ Feel lonely</td></tr>
<tr><td>☐ Feel tired</td></tr>
<tr><td>☐ Feel sad</td></tr>
<tr><td>☐ Feel neutral</td></tr>
<tr><td>☐ Am taking it minute by minute</td></tr>
</table>

I smiled when I remembered this about you... _______________________________________

____

I find it helpful when: _______________________________________

____

____

I am comforted by: _______________________________________

____

____

I feel your presence most when... _______________________________________

____

____

Whenever I start to feel overwhelmed by pain, regret or despair, I will... _____________

____

____

I will commit to this activity to help me feel better: _______________________________

____

Use this space to jot down your memory of visitations or dreams about your loved one:

____

____

____

$\mathcal{D}ate$:   /   /

If I need support today, I will call:

____

My plans for today are: _______________________________

____

____

I'm really missing this about you... _______________________

____

I smiled when I remembered this about you... ________________________________

____

I find it helpful when: ____

____

____

I am comforted by: ____

____

____

I feel your presence most when... ____________________________________

____

____

Whenever I start to feel overwhelmed by pain, regret or despair, I will... __________

____

____

I will commit to this activity to help me feel better: ____________________

____

Use this space to jot down your memory of visitations or dreams about your loved one:

____

____

____

Date: /   /

If I need support today, I will call:

____

My plans for today are: _________________________

____

____

I'm really missing this about you... _________________

____

I smiled when I remembered this about you... _______________________________

____

I find it helpful when: _________________________

____

____

I am comforted by: _________________________

____

____

I feel your presence most when... _________________________

____

____

Whenever I start to feel overwhelmed by pain, regret or despair, I will... _____________

____

____

I will commit to this activity to help me feel better: _________________________

____

Use this space to jot down your memory of visitations or dreams about your loved one:

____

____

____

Date: /   /

If I need support today, I will call:

____

My plans for today are: _______________________

____

____

I'm really missing this about you... ______________

____

I smiled when I remembered this about you... _______________________________________

____

I find it helpful when: ____

____

____

I am comforted by: ____

____

____

I feel your presence most when... ____

____

____

Whenever I start to feel overwhelmed by pain, regret or despair, I will... ______________

____

____

I will commit to this activity to help me feel better: _______________________________

____

Use this space to jot down your memory of visitations or dreams about your loved one:

____

____

____

Date: / /

If I need support today, I will call:

____

My plans for today are: _______________________

____

____

I'm really missing this about you... ________________

____

I smiled when I remembered this about you... _________________________________

____

I find it helpful when: ____

____

____

I am comforted by: ____

____

____

I feel your presence most when... ______________________________________

____

____

Whenever I start to feel overwhelmed by pain, regret or despair, I will... ____________

____

____

I will commit to this activity to help me feel better: _______________________

____

Use this space to jot down your memory of visitations or dreams about your loved one:

____

____

____

Date: /   /

If I need support today, I will call:

____

My plans for today are: ___________________________

____

____

I'm really missing this about you... ___________________

____

Today I:

☐ Feel supported
☐ Feel angry
☐ Feel like crying
☐ Feel lonely
☐ Feel tired
☐ Feel sad
☐ Feel neutral
☐ Am taking it minute by minute

I smiled when I remembered this about you... ___________________________________

____

I find it helpful when: ____

____

____

I am comforted by: ____

____

____

I feel your presence most when... ____

____

____

Whenever I start to feel overwhelmed by pain, regret or despair, I will... _____________

____

____

I will commit to this activity to help me feel better: _____________________________

____

Use this space to jot down your memory of visitations or dreams about your loved one:

____

____

____

Date: /   /

If I need support today, I will call:

____

My plans for today are: _______________________

____

____

I'm really missing this about you... _____________

I smiled when I remembered this about you... _________________________________

____

I find it helpful when: ____

____

____

I am comforted by: ____

____

____

I feel your presence most when... ____

____

____

Whenever I start to feel overwhelmed by pain, regret or despair, I will... ____________

____

____

I will commit to this activity to help me feel better: ______________________________

____

Use this space to jot down your memory of visitations or dreams about your loved one:

____

____

____

Date: /   /

If I need support today, I will call:

____

My plans for today are: _________________________

____

____

I'm really missing this about you... _______________

Today I:

- ☐ Feel supported
- ☐ Feel angry
- ☐ Feel like crying
- ☐ Feel lonely
- ☐ Feel tired
- ☐ Feel sad
- ☐ Feel neutral
- ☐ Am taking it minute by minute

I smiled when I remembered this about you... _______________________________________

____

I find it helpful when: ____

____

____

I am comforted by: ____

____

____

I feel your presence most when... ____

____

____

Whenever I start to feel overwhelmed by pain, regret or despair, I will... _______________

____

____

I will commit to this activity to help me feel better: _________________________________

____

Use this space to jot down your memory of visitations or dreams about your loved one:

____

____

____

Date: /   /

If I need support today, I will call:

____

My plans for today are: _______________________

____

____

I'm really missing this about you... ___________

I smiled when I remembered this about you... ____

____

I find it helpful when: ____

____

____

I am comforted by: ____

____

____

I feel your presence most when... ____

____

____

Whenever I start to feel overwhelmed by pain, regret or despair, I will... ______________

____

____

I will commit to this activity to help me feel better: __________________________________

____

Use this space to jot down your memory of visitations or dreams about your loved one:

____

____

____

Date: /   /

If I need support today, I will call:

____

My plans for today are: ____________________________

____

____

I'm really missing this about you... _______________________

____

I smiled when I remembered this about you... ____________________________

____

I find it helpful when: ____________________________

____

____

I am comforted by: ____________________________

____

____

I feel your presence most when... ____________________________

____

____

Whenever I start to feel overwhelmed by pain, regret or despair, I will... ____________

____

____

I will commit to this activity to help me feel better: ____________________________

____

Use this space to jot down your memory of visitations or dreams about your loved one:

____

____

____

Date: / /

If I need support today, I will call:

____

My plans for today are: _______________________

____

____

I'm really missing this about you... _______________________

____

I smiled when I remembered this about you... _______________________

____

I find it helpful when: _______________________

____

____

I am comforted by: _______________________

____

____

I feel your presence most when... _______________________

____

____

Whenever I start to feel overwhelmed by pain, regret or despair, I will... _______________________

____

____

I will commit to this activity to help me feel better: _______________________

____

Use this space to jot down your memory of visitations or dreams about your loved one:

____

____

____

If I need support today, I will call:

____

My plans for today are: _______________________

____

____

I'm really missing this about you... ________________

____

I smiled when I remembered this about you... _______________________________

____

I find it helpful when: ____

____

____

I am comforted by: ____

____

____

I feel your presence most when... _________________________________

____

____

Whenever I start to feel overwhelmed by pain, regret or despair, I will... ____________

____

____

I will commit to this activity to help me feel better: _______________________

____

Use this space to jot down your memory of visitations or dreams about your loved one:

____

____

____

Today I:

☐ Feel supported

☐ Feel angry

☐ Feel like crying

☐ Feel lonely

☐ Feel tired

☐ Feel sad

☐ Feel neutral

☐ Am taking it minute by minute

Date: /   /

If I need support today, I will call:

____

My plans for today are: _______________________

____

____

I'm really missing this about you... _______________

____

I smiled when I remembered this about you... _______________________________

____

I find it helpful when: _________________________________

____

____

I am comforted by: ___________________________________

____

____

I feel your presence most when... _______________________________

____

____

Whenever I start to feel overwhelmed by pain, regret or despair, I will... _____________

____

____

I will commit to this activity to help me feel better: _____________________

____

Use this space to jot down your memory of visitations or dreams about your loved one:

____

____

____

$Date$:   /   /

If I need support today, I will call:

____

My plans for today are: _______________________

____

____

I'm really missing this about you... ________________

Today I:

☐ Feel supported

☐ Feel angry

☐ Feel like crying

☐ Feel lonely

☐ Feel tired

☐ Feel sad

☐ Feel neutral

☐ Am taking it minute by minute

I smiled when I remembered this about you... _________________________________

____

I find it helpful when: _________________________________

____

____

I am comforted by: _________________________________

____

____

I feel your presence most when... _________________________________

____

____

Whenever I start to feel overwhelmed by pain, regret or despair, I will... _____________

____

____

I will commit to this activity to help me feel better: _________________________

____

Use this space to jot down your memory of visitations or dreams about your loved one:

____

____

____

Date: /   /

If I need support today, I will call:

____

My plans for today are: ____________________

____

____

I'm really missing this about you... ___________

____

I smiled when I remembered this about you... _______________________________________

____

I find it helpful when: ____

____

____

I am comforted by: ____

____

____

I feel your presence most when... ____

____

____

Whenever I start to feel overwhelmed by pain, regret or despair, I will... _______________

____

____

I will commit to this activity to help me feel better: ____________________________________

____

Use this space to jot down your memory of visitations or dreams about your loved one:

____

____

____

Date: / /

If I need support today, I will call:

____

My plans for today are: _________________________

____

____

I'm really missing this about you... ______________

____

I smiled when I remembered this about you... ________________________________

____

I find it helpful when: ____

____

____

I am comforted by: ____

____

____

I feel your presence most when... ____

____

____

Whenever I start to feel overwhelmed by pain, regret or despair, I will... ___________

____

____

I will commit to this activity to help me feel better: _____________________________

____

Use this space to jot down your memory of visitations or dreams about your loved one:

____

____

____

Date: /   /

If I need support today, I will call:

____

My plans for today are: ______________________________

____

____

I'm really missing this about you... ____________________

____

<table>
<tr><td>

Today I:

☐ Feel supported
☐ Feel angry
☐ Feel like crying
☐ Feel lonely
☐ Feel tired
☐ Feel sad
☐ Feel neutral
☐ Am taking it minute by minute

</td></tr>
</table>

I smiled when I remembered this about you... ____________________________________

____

I find it helpful when: ____

____

____

I am comforted by: ____

____

____

I feel your presence most when... ____

____

____

Whenever I start to feel overwhelmed by pain, regret or despair, I will... ______________

____

____

I will commit to this activity to help me feel better: _______________________________

____

Use this space to jot down your memory of visitations or dreams about your loved one:

____

____

____

If I need support today, I will call:

____

My plans for today are: _______________________

____

____

I'm really missing this about you... _____________

____

Today I:

☐ Feel supported

☐ Feel angry

☐ Feel like crying

☐ Feel lonely

☐ Feel tired

☐ Feel sad

☐ Feel neutral

☐ Am taking it minute by minute

I smiled when I remembered this about you... ____

____

I find it helpful when: ____

____

____

I am comforted by: ____

____

____

I feel your presence most when... ____

____

____

Whenever I start to feel overwhelmed by pain, regret or despair, I will... _______________

____

____

I will commit to this activity to help me feel better: _______________________________

____

Use this space to jot down your memory of visitations or dreams about your loved one:

____

____

____

Date: /   /

If I need support today, I will call:

____

My plans for today are: _______________________

____

____

I'm really missing this about you... _______________

____

I smiled when I remembered this about you... ___________________________________

____

I find it helpful when: ____

____

____

I am comforted by: ____

____

____

I feel your presence most when... ____

____

____

Whenever I start to feel overwhelmed by pain, regret or despair, I will... ___________

____

____

I will commit to this activity to help me feel better: ____________________________

____

Use this space to jot down your memory of visitations or dreams about your loved one:

____

____

____

Date: /   /

If I need support today, I will call:

____

My plans for today are: _______________________

____

____

I'm really missing this about you... _______________

____

I smiled when I remembered this about you... ______________________________________

____

I find it helpful when: ____

____

____

I am comforted by: ____

____

____

I feel your presence most when... ____

____

____

Whenever I start to feel overwhelmed by pain, regret or despair, I will... ____________

____

____

I will commit to this activity to help me feel better: _________________________

____

Use this space to jot down your memory of visitations or dreams about your loved one:

____

____

____

Date: ___ / ___ / ___

If I need support today, I will call:

____

My plans for today are: _______________________

____

____

I'm really missing this about you... ____________

I smiled when I remembered this about you... ____

____

I find it helpful when: ____

____

____

I am comforted by: ____

____

____

I feel your presence most when... ____

____

____

Whenever I start to feel overwhelmed by pain, regret or despair, I will... _______________

____

____

I will commit to this activity to help me feel better: _______________________________

____

Use this space to jot down your memory of visitations or dreams about your loved one:

____

____

____

Date: /   /

If I need support today, I will call:

____

My plans for today are: _________________________

____

____

I'm really missing this about you... _______________

____

I smiled when I remembered this about you... ____

____

I find it helpful when: ____

____

____

I am comforted by: ____

____

____

I feel your presence most when... ____

____

____

Whenever I start to feel overwhelmed by pain, regret or despair, I will... ________________

____

____

I will commit to this activity to help me feel better: ___________________________________

____

Use this space to jot down your memory of visitations or dreams about your loved one:

____

____

____

Today I:

☐ Feel supported
☐ Feel angry
☐ Feel like crying
☐ Feel lonely
☐ Feel tired
☐ Feel sad
☐ Feel neutral
☐ Am taking it minute by minute

Date: / /

If I need support today, I will call:

____

My plans for today are: _______________________________

____

____

I'm really missing this about you... _______________________

I smiled when I remembered this about you... ____

____

I find it helpful when: ____

____

____

I am comforted by: ____

____

____

I feel your presence most when... ____

____

____

Whenever I start to feel overwhelmed by pain, regret or despair, I will... _____________

____

____

I will commit to this activity to help me feel better: _______________________________

____

Use this space to jot down your memory of visitations or dreams about your loved one:

____

____

____

Date: / /

If I need support today, I will call:

____

My plans for today are: _______________________

____

____

I'm really missing this about you... _______________

____

Today I:

☐ Feel supported
☐ Feel angry
☐ Feel like crying
☐ Feel lonely
☐ Feel tired
☐ Feel sad
☐ Feel neutral
☐ Am taking it minute by minute

I smiled when I remembered this about you... _________________________________

____

I find it helpful when: ____

____

____

I am comforted by: ____

____

____

I feel your presence most when... _________________________________

____

____

Whenever I start to feel overwhelmed by pain, regret or despair, I will... _____________

____

____

I will commit to this activity to help me feel better: ____________________

____

Use this space to jot down your memory of visitations or dreams about your loved one:

____

____

____

Date: /   /

If I need support today, I will call:

____

My plans for today are: _______________________

____

____

I'm really missing this about you... ___________

____

<table>
<tr><td>Today I:</td></tr>
<tr><td>☐ Feel supported</td></tr>
<tr><td>☐ Feel angry</td></tr>
<tr><td>☐ Feel like crying</td></tr>
<tr><td>☐ Feel lonely</td></tr>
<tr><td>☐ Feel tired</td></tr>
<tr><td>☐ Feel sad</td></tr>
<tr><td>☐ Feel neutral</td></tr>
<tr><td>☐ Am taking it minute by minute</td></tr>
</table>

I smiled when I remembered this about you... ______________________________________

____

I find it helpful when: ____

____

____

I am comforted by: ____

____

____

I feel your presence most when... ____

____

____

Whenever I start to feel overwhelmed by pain, regret or despair, I will... ___________

____

____

I will commit to this activity to help me feel better: ____________________________

____

Use this space to jot down your memory of visitations or dreams about your loved one:

____

____

____

Date: /   /

If I need support today, I will call:

____

My plans for today are: _______________________________

____

____

I'm really missing this about you... _______________________

____

I smiled when I remembered this about you... ____

____

I find it helpful when: ____

____

____

I am comforted by: ____

____

____

I feel your presence most when... ____

____

____

Whenever I start to feel overwhelmed by pain, regret or despair, I will... _______________

____

____

I will commit to this activity to help me feel better: _______________________

____

Use this space to jot down your memory of visitations or dreams about your loved one:

____

____

____

<table>
<tr><td>Today I:</td></tr>
<tr><td>☐ Feel supported</td></tr>
<tr><td>☐ Feel angry</td></tr>
<tr><td>☐ Feel like crying</td></tr>
<tr><td>☐ Feel lonely</td></tr>
<tr><td>☐ Feel tired</td></tr>
<tr><td>☐ Feel sad</td></tr>
<tr><td>☐ Feel neutral</td></tr>
<tr><td>☐ Am taking it minute by minute</td></tr>
</table>

Date: /   /

If I need support today, I will call:

____

My plans for today are: _____________________________

____

____

I'm really missing this about you... _______________________

____

I smiled when I remembered this about you... _______________________________________

____

I find it helpful when: ____

____

____

I am comforted by: ____

____

____

I feel your presence most when... _________________________________

____

____

Whenever I start to feel overwhelmed by pain, regret or despair, I will... _____________

____

____

I will commit to this activity to help me feel better: _____________________

____

Use this space to jot down your memory of visitations or dreams about your loved one:

____

____

____

Date: /   /

If I need support today, I will call:

____

My plans for today are: _______________________

____

____

I'm really missing this about you... _____________

____

I smiled when I remembered this about you... ____

____

I find it helpful when: ____

____

____

I am comforted by: ____

____

____

I feel your presence most when... ____

____

____

Whenever I start to feel overwhelmed by pain, regret or despair, I will... _______________

____

____

I will commit to this activity to help me feel better: ________________________________

____

Use this space to jot down your memory of visitations or dreams about your loved one:

____

____

____

Date: /   /

If I need support today, I will call:

____

My plans for today are: _________________________

____

____

I'm really missing this about you... _______________

I smiled when I remembered this about you... ____

____

I find it helpful when: ____

____

____

I am comforted by: ____

____

____

I feel your presence most when... ____

____

____

Whenever I start to feel overwhelmed by pain, regret or despair, I will... __________________

____

____

I will commit to this activity to help me feel better: ______________________________________

____

Use this space to jot down your memory of visitations or dreams about your loved one:

____

____

____

Date: /   /

If I need support today, I will call:

____

My plans for today are: _______________________________

____

____

I'm really missing this about you... _______________________

____

I smiled when I remembered this about you... _______________________________

____

I find it helpful when: _______________________________________

____

____

I am comforted by: ____

____

____

I feel your presence most when... _________________________________

____

____

Whenever I start to feel overwhelmed by pain, regret or despair, I will... ____________

____

____

I will commit to this activity to help me feel better: ____________________

____

Use this space to jot down your memory of visitations or dreams about your loved one:

____

____

____

Date: ___/___/___

If I need support today, I will call:

____

My plans for today are: _______________________

____

____

I'm really missing this about you... _____________

____

I smiled when I remembered this about you... _________________________________

____

I find it helpful when: _________________________

____

____

I am comforted by: ___________________________

____

____

I feel your presence most when... ________________

____

____

Whenever I start to feel overwhelmed by pain, regret or despair, I will... _____________

____

____

I will commit to this activity to help me feel better: _______________________

____

Use this space to jot down your memory of visitations or dreams about your loved one:

____

____

____

Date: /   /

If I need support today, I will call:

____

My plans for today are: ____________________________

____

____

I'm really missing this about you... _________________

____

I smiled when I remembered this about you... _______________________________________

____

I find it helpful when: ____

____

____

I am comforted by: ____

____

____

I feel your presence most when... ____

____

____

Whenever I start to feel overwhelmed by pain, regret or despair, I will... ____________

____

____

I will commit to this activity to help me feel better: _______________________________

____

Use this space to jot down your memory of visitations or dreams about your loved one:

____

____

____

Date: / /

If I need support today, I will call:

____

My plans for today are: _______________________

____

____

I'm really missing this about you... _______________

I smiled when I remembered this about you... _______________________________

____

I find it helpful when: _______________________________

____

____

I am comforted by: _______________________________

____

____

I feel your presence most when... _______________________________

____

____

Whenever I start to feel overwhelmed by pain, regret or despair, I will... _____________

____

____

I will commit to this activity to help me feel better: _______________________

____

Use this space to jot down your memory of visitations or dreams about your loved one:

____

____

____

$Date:$ /   /

If I need support today, I will call:

____

My plans for today are: _______________________

____

____

I'm really missing this about you... _______________

____

<table>
<tr><td>Today I:</td></tr>
<tr><td>☐ Feel supported</td></tr>
<tr><td>☐ Feel angry</td></tr>
<tr><td>☐ Feel like crying</td></tr>
<tr><td>☐ Feel lonely</td></tr>
<tr><td>☐ Feel tired</td></tr>
<tr><td>☐ Feel sad</td></tr>
<tr><td>☐ Feel neutral</td></tr>
<tr><td>☐ Am taking it minute by minute</td></tr>
</table>

I smiled when I remembered this about you... _______________________________________

____

I find it helpful when: ____

____

____

I am comforted by: ____

____

____

I feel your presence most when... ____

____

____

Whenever I start to feel overwhelmed by pain, regret or despair, I will... _______________

____

____

I will commit to this activity to help me feel better: ________________________________

____

Use this space to jot down your memory of visitations or dreams about your loved one:

____

____

____

Date: / /

If I need support today, I will call:

____

My plans for today are: ______________________

____

____

I'm really missing this about you... ________________

I smiled when I remembered this about you... ____________________________________

____

I find it helpful when: _______________________________________

____

____

I am comforted by: ____

____

____

I feel your presence most when... ____________________________________

____

____

Whenever I start to feel overwhelmed by pain, regret or despair, I will... _____________

____

____

I will commit to this activity to help me feel better: ______________________________

____

Use this space to jot down your memory of visitations or dreams about your loved one:

____

____

____

$\mathcal{D}ate$: /   /

If I need support today, I will call:

____

My plans for today are: _______________________________

____

____

I'm really missing this about you... _________________________

<table>
<tr><td>Today I:</td></tr>
<tr><td>☐ Feel supported</td></tr>
<tr><td>☐ Feel angry</td></tr>
<tr><td>☐ Feel like crying</td></tr>
<tr><td>☐ Feel lonely</td></tr>
<tr><td>☐ Feel tired</td></tr>
<tr><td>☐ Feel sad</td></tr>
<tr><td>☐ Feel neutral</td></tr>
<tr><td>☐ Am taking it minute by minute</td></tr>
</table>

I smiled when I remembered this about you... ____________________________________

____

I find it helpful when: ____

____

____

I am comforted by: ____

____

____

I feel your presence most when... ____

____

____

Whenever I start to feel overwhelmed by pain, regret or despair, I will... ___________

____

____

I will commit to this activity to help me feel better: ______________________________

____

Use this space to jot down your memory of visitations or dreams about your loved one:

____

____

____

Date: /   /

If I need support today, I will call:

____

My plans for today are: ____________________________

____

____

I'm really missing this about you... _________________

____

I smiled when I remembered this about you... __________________________________

____

I find it helpful when: ____

____

____

I am comforted by: ____

____

____

I feel your presence most when... ____

____

____

Whenever I start to feel overwhelmed by pain, regret or despair, I will... ____________

____

____

I will commit to this activity to help me feel better: _________________________

____

Use this space to jot down your memory of visitations or dreams about your loved one:

____

____

____

Date: /   /

If I need support today, I will call:

____

My plans for today are: _______________________

____

____

I'm really missing this about you... ___________

____

I smiled when I remembered this about you... _______________________________________

____

I find it helpful when: ____

____

____

I am comforted by: ____

____

____

I feel your presence most when... ____

____

____

Whenever I start to feel overwhelmed by pain, regret or despair, I will... ______________

____

____

I will commit to this activity to help me feel better: ____________________________

____

Use this space to jot down your memory of visitations or dreams about your loved one:

____

____

____

Date: / /

If I need support today, I will call:

____

My plans for today are: _______________________________

____

____

I'm really missing this about you... _______________________

I smiled when I remembered this about you... _______________________________

____

I find it helpful when: _________________________________

____

____

I am comforted by: ___________________________________

____

____

I feel your presence most when... ___________________________

____

____

Whenever I start to feel overwhelmed by pain, regret or despair, I will... ___________

____

____

I will commit to this activity to help me feel better: _____________________

____

Use this space to jot down your memory of visitations or dreams about your loved one:

____

____

____

Date: /   /

If I need support today, I will call:

____

My plans for today are: ___________________________

____

____

I'm really missing this about you... __________________

____

I smiled when I remembered this about you... _______________________________________

____

I find it helpful when: ____

____

____

I am comforted by: ____

____

____

I feel your presence most when... ____

____

____

Whenever I start to feel overwhelmed by pain, regret or despair, I will... _______________

____

____

I will commit to this activity to help me feel better: __________________________________

____

Use this space to jot down your memory of visitations or dreams about your loved one:

____

____

____

Date: /   /

If I need support today, I will call:

____

My plans for today are: _______________________________

____

____

I'm really missing this about you... _______________________

I smiled when I remembered this about you... _____________________________________

____

I find it helpful when: ____

____

____

I am comforted by: ____

____

____

I feel your presence most when... ____

____

____

Whenever I start to feel overwhelmed by pain, regret or despair, I will... _____________

____

____

I will commit to this activity to help me feel better: _________________________

____

Use this space to jot down your memory of visitations or dreams about your loved one:

____

____

____

Date: / /

If I need support today, I will call:

____

My plans for today are: _______________________

____

____

I'm really missing this about you... _____________

____

I smiled when I remembered this about you... _______________________________

____

I find it helpful when: ____

____

____

I am comforted by: ____

____

____

I feel your presence most when... ____

____

____

Whenever I start to feel overwhelmed by pain, regret or despair, I will... ___________

____

____

I will commit to this activity to help me feel better: _________________________

____

Use this space to jot down your memory of visitations or dreams about your loved one:

____

____

____

Date: /   /

If I need support today, I will call:

____

My plans for today are: _______________________

____

____

I'm really missing this about you... ____________

____

I smiled when I remembered this about you... ____

____

I find it helpful when: ____

____

____

I am comforted by: ____

____

____

I feel your presence most when... ____

____

____

Whenever I start to feel overwhelmed by pain, regret or despair, I will... ______________

____

____

I will commit to this activity to help me feel better: _________________________________

____

Use this space to jot down your memory of visitations or dreams about your loved one:

____

____

____

$\mathcal{D}$ate: / /

Today I:

☐ Feel supported
☐ Feel angry
☐ Feel like crying
☐ Feel lonely
☐ Feel tired
☐ Feel sad
☐ Feel neutral
☐ Am taking it minute by minute

If I need support today, I will call:

____

My plans for today are: _____________________________

____

____

I'm really missing this about you... _____________________

____

I smiled when I remembered this about you... ____

____

I find it helpful when: ____

____

____

I am comforted by: ____

____

____

I feel your presence most when... ____

____

____

Whenever I start to feel overwhelmed by pain, regret or despair, I will... _____________

____

____

I will commit to this activity to help me feel better: _______________________________

____

Use this space to jot down your memory of visitations or dreams about your loved one:

____

____

____

$\mathcal{D}ate$:   /   /

If I need support today, I will call:

____

My plans for today are: _______________________

____

____

I'm really missing this about you... ____________

Today I:
☐ Feel supported
☐ Feel angry
☐ Feel like crying
☐ Feel lonely
☐ Feel tired
☐ Feel sad
☐ Feel neutral
☐ Am taking it minute by minute

I smiled when I remembered this about you... ____________________________________

____

I find it helpful when: _________________________

____

____

I am comforted by: ____________________________

____

____

I feel your presence most when... _______________

____

____

Whenever I start to feel overwhelmed by pain, regret or despair, I will... __________

____

____

I will commit to this activity to help me feel better: ____________________

____

Use this space to jot down your memory of visitations or dreams about your loved one:

____

____

____

Date: /   /

If I need support today, I will call:

____

My plans for today are: _______________________________

____

____

I'm really missing this about you... _______________________

____

I smiled when I remembered this about you... _______________________________________

____

I find it helpful when: _______________________________________

____

____

I am comforted by: _______________________________________

____

____

I feel your presence most when... _______________________________________

____

____

Whenever I start to feel overwhelmed by pain, regret or despair, I will... _______________

____

____

I will commit to this activity to help me feel better: _______________________

____

Use this space to jot down your memory of visitations or dreams about your loved one:

____

____

____

Today I:

☐ Feel supported

☐ Feel angry

☐ Feel like crying

☐ Feel lonely

☐ Feel tired

☐ Feel sad

☐ Feel neutral

☐ Am taking it minute by minute

Date: / /

If I need support today, I will call:

____

My plans for today are: _______________________

____

____

I'm really missing this about you... _______________

I smiled when I remembered this about you... _______________________________________

____

I find it helpful when: _______________________________________

____

____

I am comforted by: _______________________________________

____

____

I feel your presence most when... _______________________________________

____

____

Whenever I start to feel overwhelmed by pain, regret or despair, I will... _______________

____

____

I will commit to this activity to help me feel better: _______________________________________

____

Use this space to jot down your memory of visitations or dreams about your loved one:

____

____

____

Date: /   /

If I need support today, I will call:

____

My plans for today are: _______________________________

____

____

I'm really missing this about you... _____________________

____

I smiled when I remembered this about you... ____

____

I find it helpful when: ____

____

____

I am comforted by: ____

____

____

I feel your presence most when... _______________________________________

____

____

Whenever I start to feel overwhelmed by pain, regret or despair, I will... ____________

____

____

I will commit to this activity to help me feel better: _____________________________

____

Use this space to jot down your memory of visitations or dreams about your loved one:

____

____

____

Date: /   /

If I need support today, I will call:

____

My plans for today are: _________________________

____

____

I'm really missing this about you... _______________

____

I smiled when I remembered this about you... ______________________________________

____

I find it helpful when: ____

____

____

I am comforted by: ____

____

____

I feel your presence most when... ____

____

____

Whenever I start to feel overwhelmed by pain, regret or despair, I will... _______________

____

____

I will commit to this activity to help me feel better: _________________________________

____

Use this space to jot down your memory of visitations or dreams about your loved one:

____

____

____

Date: /   /

If I need support today, I will call:

____

My plans for today are: ______________________________

____

____

I'm really missing this about you... _______________________

____

<table>
<tr><td>Today I:</td></tr>
<tr><td>☐ Feel supported</td></tr>
<tr><td>☐ Feel angry</td></tr>
<tr><td>☐ Feel like crying</td></tr>
<tr><td>☐ Feel lonely</td></tr>
<tr><td>☐ Feel tired</td></tr>
<tr><td>☐ Feel sad</td></tr>
<tr><td>☐ Feel neutral</td></tr>
<tr><td>☐ Am taking it minute by minute</td></tr>
</table>

I smiled when I remembered this about you... _______________________________

____

I find it helpful when: _______________________________________

____

____

I am comforted by: ____

____

____

I feel your presence most when... ____________________________________

____

____

Whenever I start to feel overwhelmed by pain, regret or despair, I will... _____________

____

____

I will commit to this activity to help me feel better: ____________________________

____

Use this space to jot down your memory of visitations or dreams about your loved one:

____

____

____

Date: /   /

If I need support today, I will call:

____

My plans for today are: _________________________

____

____

I'm really missing this about you... ______________

I smiled when I remembered this about you... ____

____

I find it helpful when: ____

____

____

I am comforted by: ____

____

____

I feel your presence most when... ____

____

____

Whenever I start to feel overwhelmed by pain, regret or despair, I will... _______________

____

____

I will commit to this activity to help me feel better: _________________________________

____

Use this space to jot down your memory of visitations or dreams about your loved one:

____

____

____

Date: /   /

If I need support today, I will call:

____

My plans for today are: _______________________

____

____

I'm really missing this about you... _______________

____

I smiled when I remembered this about you... _________________________________

____

I find it helpful when: ____

____

____

I am comforted by: ____

____

____

I feel your presence most when... ____

____

____

Whenever I start to feel overwhelmed by pain, regret or despair, I will... ___________

____

____

I will commit to this activity to help me feel better: _______________________

____

Use this space to jot down your memory of visitations or dreams about your loved one:

____

____

____

Date: / /

If I need support today, I will call:

____

My plans for today are: _______________________

____

____

I'm really missing this about you... _______________

____

I smiled when I remembered this about you... ____

____

I find it helpful when: ___________________________

____

____

I am comforted by: ______________________________

____

____

I feel your presence most when... _________________

____

____

Whenever I start to feel overwhelmed by pain, regret or despair, I will... _______________

____

____

I will commit to this activity to help me feel better: _______________

____

Use this space to jot down your memory of visitations or dreams about your loved one:

____

____

____

Date: / /

If I need support today, I will call:

____

My plans for today are: _______________________

____

____

I'm really missing this about you... _______________

____

I smiled when I remembered this about you... _______________________________

____

I find it helpful when: ___________________________________

____

____

I am comforted by: _____________________________________

____

____

I feel your presence most when... _________________________________

____

____

Whenever I start to feel overwhelmed by pain, regret or despair, I will... _____________

____

____

I will commit to this activity to help me feel better: _____________________

____

Use this space to jot down your memory of visitations or dreams about your loved one:

____

____

____

Date: ___ / ___ / ___

If I need support today, I will call:

____

My plans for today are: ___________________

____

____

I'm really missing this about you... ___________

____

I smiled when I remembered this about you... ____

____

I find it helpful when: ____

____

____

I am comforted by: ____

____

____

I feel your presence most when... ____

____

____

Whenever I start to feel overwhelmed by pain, regret or despair, I will... _______________

____

____

I will commit to this activity to help me feel better: _________________________________

____

Use this space to jot down your memory of visitations or dreams about your loved one:

____

____

____

Date: /   /

If I need support today, I will call:

____

My plans for today are: _______________________

____

____

I'm really missing this about you... ____________

____

<table>
<tr><td>Today I:</td></tr>
<tr><td>☐ Feel supported</td></tr>
<tr><td>☐ Feel angry</td></tr>
<tr><td>☐ Feel like crying</td></tr>
<tr><td>☐ Feel lonely</td></tr>
<tr><td>☐ Feel tired</td></tr>
<tr><td>☐ Feel sad</td></tr>
<tr><td>☐ Feel neutral</td></tr>
<tr><td>☐ Am taking it minute by minute</td></tr>
</table>

I smiled when I remembered this about you... _______________________________________

____

I find it helpful when: ____

____

____

I am comforted by: ____

____

____

I feel your presence most when... ____

____

____

Whenever I start to feel overwhelmed by pain, regret or despair, I will... ________________

____

____

I will commit to this activity to help me feel better: __________________________________

____

Use this space to jot down your memory of visitations or dreams about your loved one:

____

____

____

Date: / /

If I need support today, I will call:

____

My plans for today are: ______________________________

____

____

I'm really missing this about you... ______________________

____

I smiled when I remembered this about you... ________________________________

____

I find it helpful when: ____

____

____

I am comforted by: ____________________________________

____

____

I feel your presence most when... ____________________________________

____

____

Whenever I start to feel overwhelmed by pain, regret or despair, I will... ____________

____

____

I will commit to this activity to help me feel better: ____________________________

____

Use this space to jot down your memory of visitations or dreams about your loved one:

____

____

____

Date: /   /

If I need support today, I will call:

____

My plans for today are: _______________________________

____

____

I'm really missing this about you... _______________________

____

I smiled when I remembered this about you... _________________________________

____

I find it helpful when: _______________________________________

____

____

I am comforted by: ____

____

____

I feel your presence most when... _______________________________

____

____

Whenever I start to feel overwhelmed by pain, regret or despair, I will... ____________

____

____

I will commit to this activity to help me feel better: _____________________

____

Use this space to jot down your memory of visitations or dreams about your loved one:

____

____

____

Date: /   /

If I need support today, I will call:

____

My plans for today are: _______________________________

____

____

I'm really missing this about you... ____________________

I smiled when I remembered this about you... ____________________________________

____

I find it helpful when: ____

____

____

I am comforted by: ____

____

____

I feel your presence most when... _________________________________

____

____

Whenever I start to feel overwhelmed by pain, regret or despair, I will... ___________

____

____

I will commit to this activity to help me feel better: _______________________

____

Use this space to jot down your memory of visitations or dreams about your loved one:

____

____

____

Date: /   /

If I need support today, I will call:

____

My plans for today are: _______________________________

____

____

I'm really missing this about you... _______________________

I smiled when I remembered this about you... ____

____

I find it helpful when: ____

____

____

I am comforted by: ____

____

____

I feel your presence most when... ____

____

____

Whenever I start to feel overwhelmed by pain, regret or despair, I will... _______________

____

____

I will commit to this activity to help me feel better: _______________________________

____

Use this space to jot down your memory of visitations or dreams about your loved one:

____

____

____

Date: /   /

If I need support today, I will call:

____

My plans for today are: _________________________

____

____

I'm really missing this about you... _______________

____

I smiled when I remembered this about you... ____

____

I find it helpful when: ____

____

____

I am comforted by: ____

____

____

I feel your presence most when... ____

____

____

Whenever I start to feel overwhelmed by pain, regret or despair, I will... ______________

____

____

I will commit to this activity to help me feel better: _________________________________

____

Use this space to jot down your memory of visitations or dreams about your loved one:

____

____

____

Today I:
☐ Feel supported
☐ Feel angry
☐ Feel like crying
☐ Feel lonely
☐ Feel tired
☐ Feel sad
☐ Feel neutral
☐ Am taking it minute by minute

Date: _____ / _____ / _____

If I need support today, I will call:

____

My plans for today are: _______________________

____

____

I'm really missing this about you... _______________

____

<table>
<tr><td>Today I:</td></tr>
<tr><td>☐ Feel supported</td></tr>
<tr><td>☐ Feel angry</td></tr>
<tr><td>☐ Feel like crying</td></tr>
<tr><td>☐ Feel lonely</td></tr>
<tr><td>☐ Feel tired</td></tr>
<tr><td>☐ Feel sad</td></tr>
<tr><td>☐ Feel neutral</td></tr>
<tr><td>☐ Am taking it minute by minute</td></tr>
</table>

I smiled when I remembered this about you... _______________________________________

____

I find it helpful when: ____

____

____

I am comforted by: ____

____

____

I feel your presence most when... ____

____

____

Whenever I start to feel overwhelmed by pain, regret or despair, I will... _______________

____

____

I will commit to this activity to help me feel better: _______________________________

____

Use this space to jot down your memory of visitations or dreams about your loved one:

____

____

____

Date: / /

If I need support today, I will call:

____

My plans for today are: ________________________

____

____

I'm really missing this about you... ____________

____

I smiled when I remembered this about you... ____

____

I find it helpful when: ____

____

____

I am comforted by: ____

____

____

I feel your presence most when... ____

____

____

Whenever I start to feel overwhelmed by pain, regret or despair, I will... _______________

____

____

I will commit to this activity to help me feel better: ___________________________________

____

Use this space to jot down your memory of visitations or dreams about your loved one:

____

____

____

Date: /   /

If I need support today, I will call:

____

My plans for today are: ____________________________

____

____

I'm really missing this about you... ____________________

____

I smiled when I remembered this about you... ________________________

____

I find it helpful when: ________________________________

____

____

I am comforted by: ___________________________________

____

____

I feel your presence most when... ______________________

____

____

Whenever I start to feel overwhelmed by pain, regret or despair, I will... __________

____

____

I will commit to this activity to help me feel better: ______________

____

Use this space to jot down your memory of visitations or dreams about your loved one:

____

____

____

Date: /   /

If I need support today, I will call:

____

My plans for today are: _________________________

____

____

I'm really missing this about you... _______________

I smiled when I remembered this about you... ____

____

I find it helpful when: ____

____

____

I am comforted by: ____

____

____

I feel your presence most when... ____

____

____

Whenever I start to feel overwhelmed by pain, regret or despair, I will... ________________

____

____

I will commit to this activity to help me feel better: _________________________________

____

Use this space to jot down your memory of visitations or dreams about your loved one:

____

____

____

Date: /   /

If I need support today, I will call:

____

My plans for today are: _______________________

____

____

I'm really missing this about you... _______________

____

I smiled when I remembered this about you... _______________________________________

____

I find it helpful when: ____

____

____

I am comforted by: ____

____

____

I feel your presence most when... ____

____

____

Whenever I start to feel overwhelmed by pain, regret or despair, I will... _____________

____

____

I will commit to this activity to help me feel better: _________________________________

____

Use this space to jot down your memory of visitations or dreams about your loved one:

____

____

____

Date: ___ / ___ / ___

If I need support today, I will call:

____

My plans for today are: _______________________

____

____

I'm really missing this about you... _______________

____

I smiled when I remembered this about you... _______________________________________

____

I find it helpful when: ____

____

____

I am comforted by: ____

____

____

I feel your presence most when... ____

____

____

Whenever I start to feel overwhelmed by pain, regret or despair, I will... _____________

____

____

I will commit to this activity to help me feel better: _______________________________

____

Use this space to jot down your memory of visitations or dreams about your loved one:

____

____

____

$Date$: ___ / ___ / ___

If I need support today, I will call:

____

My plans for today are: _______________________

____

____

I'm really missing this about you... _______________

____

Today I:

☐ Feel supported

☐ Feel angry

☐ Feel like crying

☐ Feel lonely

☐ Feel tired

☐ Feel sad

☐ Feel neutral

☐ Am taking it minute by minute

I smiled when I remembered this about you... ______________________________

____

I find it helpful when: ________________________________

____

____

I am comforted by: __________________________________

____

____

I feel your presence most when... ____________________________

____

____

Whenever I start to feel overwhelmed by pain, regret or despair, I will... __________

____

____

I will commit to this activity to help me feel better: ____________________

____

Use this space to jot down your memory of visitations or dreams about your loved one:

____

____

____

Date: /   /

If I need support today, I will call:

____

My plans for today are: _________________________

____

____

I'm really missing this about you... ______________

____

I smiled when I remembered this about you... _______________________________

____

I find it helpful when: _______________________________

____

____

I am comforted by: _______________________________

____

____

I feel your presence most when... _______________________________

____

____

Whenever I start to feel overwhelmed by pain, regret or despair, I will... ___________

____

____

I will commit to this activity to help me feel better: ___________________________

____

Use this space to jot down your memory of visitations or dreams about your loved one:

____

____

____

Date: /   /

If I need support today, I will call:

____

My plans for today are: _______________________

____

____

I'm really missing this about you... _____________

____

<table>
<tr><td>Today I:</td></tr>
<tr><td>☐ Feel supported</td></tr>
<tr><td>☐ Feel angry</td></tr>
<tr><td>☐ Feel like crying</td></tr>
<tr><td>☐ Feel lonely</td></tr>
<tr><td>☐ Feel tired</td></tr>
<tr><td>☐ Feel sad</td></tr>
<tr><td>☐ Feel neutral</td></tr>
<tr><td>☐ Am taking it minute by minute</td></tr>
</table>

I smiled when I remembered this about you... _______________________________________

____

I find it helpful when: ____

____

____

I am comforted by: ____

____

____

I feel your presence most when... ____

____

____

Whenever I start to feel overwhelmed by pain, regret or despair, I will... _____________

____

____

I will commit to this activity to help me feel better: ___________________________

____

Use this space to jot down your memory of visitations or dreams about your loved one:

____

____

____

Date: ___ / ___ / ___

If I need support today, I will call:

____

My plans for today are: ____________________

____

____

I'm really missing this about you... ____________

I smiled when I remembered this about you... ________________________________

____

I find it helpful when: _______________________________________

____

____

I am comforted by: ____

____

____

I feel your presence most when... ________________________________

____

____

Whenever I start to feel overwhelmed by pain, regret or despair, I will... ____________

____

____

I will commit to this activity to help me feel better: ____________________________

____

Use this space to jot down your memory of visitations or dreams about your loved one:

____

____

____

Date: / /

If I need support today, I will call:

____

My plans for today are: _______________________________

____

____

I'm really missing this about you... ________________________

____

I smiled when I remembered this about you... ___________________________________

____

I find it helpful when: ____

____

____

I am comforted by: ____

____

____

I feel your presence most when... _________________________________

____

____

Whenever I start to feel overwhelmed by pain, regret or despair, I will... _____________

____

____

I will commit to this activity to help me feel better: _______________________

____

Use this space to jot down your memory of visitations or dreams about your loved one:

____

____

____

Date: ___ / ___ / ___

If I need support today, I will call:

____

My plans for today are: _______________________

____

____

I'm really missing this about you... _______________

____

I smiled when I remembered this about you... _______________________________________

____

I find it helpful when: _______________________________________

____

____

I am comforted by: _______________________________________

____

____

I feel your presence most when... _______________________________________

____

____

Whenever I start to feel overwhelmed by pain, regret or despair, I will... _______________

____

____

I will commit to this activity to help me feel better: _______________________________________

____

Use this space to jot down your memory of visitations or dreams about your loved one:

____

____

____

$Date$: ___ / ___ / ___

If I need support today, I will call:

____

My plans for today are: ______________________

____

____

I'm really missing this about you... ______________

____

I smiled when I remembered this about you... ______________________________________

____

I find it helpful when: ______________________________________

____

____

I am comforted by: ______________________________________

____

____

I feel your presence most when... ______________________________________

____

____

Whenever I start to feel overwhelmed by pain, regret or despair, I will... ______________

____

____

I will commit to this activity to help me feel better: ______________________________________

____

Use this space to jot down your memory of visitations or dreams about your loved one:

____

____

____

Date: /   /

If I need support today, I will call:

____

My plans for today are: ____________________________________

____

____

I'm really missing this about you... ____________________________

____

I smiled when I remembered this about you... _____________________________________

____

I find it helpful when: ____

____

____

I am comforted by: ____

____

____

I feel your presence most when... ____

____

____

Whenever I start to feel overwhelmed by pain, regret or despair, I will... ____________

____

____

I will commit to this activity to help me feel better: ___________________________

____

Use this space to jot down your memory of visitations or dreams about your loved one:

____

____

____

Date: /   /

If I need support today, I will call:

____

My plans for today are: _________________________

____

____

I'm really missing this about you... ______________

I smiled when I remembered this about you... ___________________________________

____

I find it helpful when: ___________________________________

____

____

I am comforted by: ___________________________________

____

____

I feel your presence most when... ___________________________________

____

____

Whenever I start to feel overwhelmed by pain, regret or despair, I will... ___________

____

____

I will commit to this activity to help me feel better: ___________________________

____

Use this space to jot down your memory of visitations or dreams about your loved one:

____

____

____

Date: /   /

If I need support today, I will call:

____

My plans for today are: ______________________________

____

____

I'm really missing this about you... ____________________

____

I smiled when I remembered this about you... ________________________

____

I find it helpful when: ______________________________

____

____

I am comforted by: ______________________________

____

____

I feel your presence most when... ______________________

____

____

Whenever I start to feel overwhelmed by pain, regret or despair, I will... ____________

____

____

I will commit to this activity to help me feel better: ______________________

____

Use this space to jot down your memory of visitations or dreams about your loved one:

____

____

____

$\mathcal{D}ate$:   /   /

If I need support today, I will call:

____

My plans for today are: _______________________________

____

____

I'm really missing this about you... _______________________

____

<table>
<tr><td>Today I:</td></tr>
<tr><td>☐ Feel supported</td></tr>
<tr><td>☐ Feel angry</td></tr>
<tr><td>☐ Feel like crying</td></tr>
<tr><td>☐ Feel lonely</td></tr>
<tr><td>☐ Feel tired</td></tr>
<tr><td>☐ Feel sad</td></tr>
<tr><td>☐ Feel neutral</td></tr>
<tr><td>☐ Am taking it minute by minute</td></tr>
</table>

I smiled when I remembered this about you... _____________________________________

____

I find it helpful when: ____

____

____

I am comforted by: ____

____

____

I feel your presence most when... ____

____

____

Whenever I start to feel overwhelmed by pain, regret or despair, I will... _____________

____

____

I will commit to this activity to help me feel better: ________________________

____

Use this space to jot down your memory of visitations or dreams about your loved one:

____

____

____

Date: /   /

If I need support today, I will call:

____

My plans for today are: _________________________

____

____

I'm really missing this about you... _______________

I smiled when I remembered this about you... ____

____

I find it helpful when: ____

____

____

I am comforted by: ____

____

____

I feel your presence most when... ____

____

____

Whenever I start to feel overwhelmed by pain, regret or despair, I will... ______________

____

____

I will commit to this activity to help me feel better: __________________________________

____

Use this space to jot down your memory of visitations or dreams about your loved one:

____

____

____

Date: / /

If I need support today, I will call:

____

My plans for today are: _______________________

____

____

I'm really missing this about you... _____________

I smiled when I remembered this about you... _______________________________________

____

I find it helpful when: ____

____

____

I am comforted by: ____

____

____

I feel your presence most when... ____

____

____

Whenever I start to feel overwhelmed by pain, regret or despair, I will... _____________

____

____

I will commit to this activity to help me feel better: _______________________________

____

Use this space to jot down your memory of visitations or dreams about your loved one:

____

____

____

I will honor your legacy by:

I will honor your legacy by:

I will honor your legacy by:

25 ways TO KEEP YOUR LOVED ONE'S SPIRIT ALIVE AFTER THEY HAVE TRANSITIONED

1. Talk about your loved one daily
2. Write down your thoughts about your loved one as they occur to you
3. Record your dreams about your departed loved one
4. Wear their favorite color
5. Dine at their favorite restaurant on a special occasion
6. Memorialize and update their social media pages
7. Plant a tree
8. Organize a balloon release on special occasions
9. Visit their final resting spot frequently
10. Stay in contact with your loved one's closest friends and exchange memories
11. Create photo pillows and blankets with their image
12. Complete things they wanted to complete but they did not complete (I wrote and released a published book because my mom always wanted to be a published author)
13. Create and maintain a garden of their favorite fruits or vegetables
14. Honor their spirit during special occasions by placing a single rose in a chair honoring their spiritual presence
15. Celebrate/Acknowledge their heavenly birthdays
16. Commit Random Acts of Kindness
17. Create social media groups & exchange memories with others who have lost loved ones
18. Burn their favorite scented candles
19. Create a sacred box that includes precious items of your loved one
20. Name your child after your loved one
21. Go on a vacation that your loved one always wanted to go on
22. Walk on the beach barefoot and allow beautiful memories to flow about your loved one
23. Donate to their favorite charity/organization
24. Ask their favorite employer to create and hang a memorial plaque
25. Wear jewelry that reminds you of your loved one (I wear bee jewelry to feel close to my mom's spirit since I always called her Miss Bee)

There is no right or wrong way to honor your loved one's legacy or how to keep their spirit alive.

Whatever you do, don't abandon their spirit.

Kinyatta E. Gray is the CEO of FlightsInStilettos, LLC, The Stylish Writing Center founder, and a published author.

Instagram
@the_stylish_writing_center

Websites
https://www.flightsinstilettos.com/
https://www.etsy.com/shop/StylishWritingCenter

Disclaimer: Kinyatta E. Gray is not a mental health provider and is providing this information based on real-life experience and to inspire others to keep their loved one's legacy alive. If you are experiencing a physical or emotional crisis, seek the help of a mental health professional.

OTHER GUIDED JOURNALS & DIARIES *by* KINYATTA E. GRAY

I Miss You...

Daily Writing Prompts for Reflection, Remembrance, and Spirit Renewal

Sexy Baby Mama

Self-Love | Self-Reflections | Spirit Renewal

Fashionista's Travel Diary

A Guided Travel Diary for Travel Planning & Reflections

The "Hallelujah" Notes

Sunday Worship Notes & Reflections

I'm Doing Me

The Ultimate Breakup Diary for Venting, Reflection & Spirit Renewal

Caring for Every Inch of Me

Daily Reflections for Self-Care & Spirit Renewal

While I'm Still Here

A Guided Expression Journal of Life, Love and Legacy for Those Preparing to Transition

Chapter 30

Capturing Life, Love & Lessons in my 30s

My Crazy Teenage Life

The Ultimate Expression Diary for Venting, Self-Reflections and Self-Love

Chapter 40

Capturing Life, Love & Lessons in my 40s

I Am A Man. I Have Feelings.

A Guided 90-Day Self-Reflections & Gratitude Journal for Men

Chapter 50

Capturing Life, Love & Lessons in my 50s

The Queen's Manifestation Journal

Daily Writing Prompt for Manifesting the Life You Want

Remembering Mom

A Grief Journal for Reflections and Remembrance

Budget & Shop

A Monthly Personal Budget & Expense Tracker for Young Adults

Men Have Feelings Too

A Guided 60-day. Self-Reflections, Self-Care & Gratitude Journal for Men

My Life My Love My Truth

LGBTQ journal

I miss you. I love you. I'm taking it day by day
for as long as it takes.

Kinyatta E. Gray

AUTHOR & CELEBRITY TRAVEL INFLUENCER